Crystal Goes to Sturgis

Written by Audrey Gibbons

Illustrated by Ruth Carney Fox

Text copyright © 2015 by Audrey Gibbons

Illustration copyright © Ruth Carney Fox

First printing, 2015
First in the Series of TripTownBooks

All rights reserved. No part of this publication may be
reproduced, distributed, or transmitted in any form or by any means,
including photocopying, recording, or other electronic or mechanical methods,
without the prior written permission of the author.
For permission requests, write to the address below.

TripTownBooks
55 Bear Tracks Hill Rd
Seward, PA 15954
Tagib684@verizon.net

ISBN-10: 0-578-16133-8
ISBN-13: 978-0-578-16133-4

Printed in the United States of America
Valley Printing and Design
667 Main Street
Johnstown, PA 15901

Dedicated to

All of the old riders from our past,

the riders of the present,

and the young riders of the future.

In Memory of

Kevin Henry

1964-2010

Sturgis this way

Crystal loves motorcycles.

She daydreams about motorcycles.

She even pretends that her bicycle is a motorcycle.

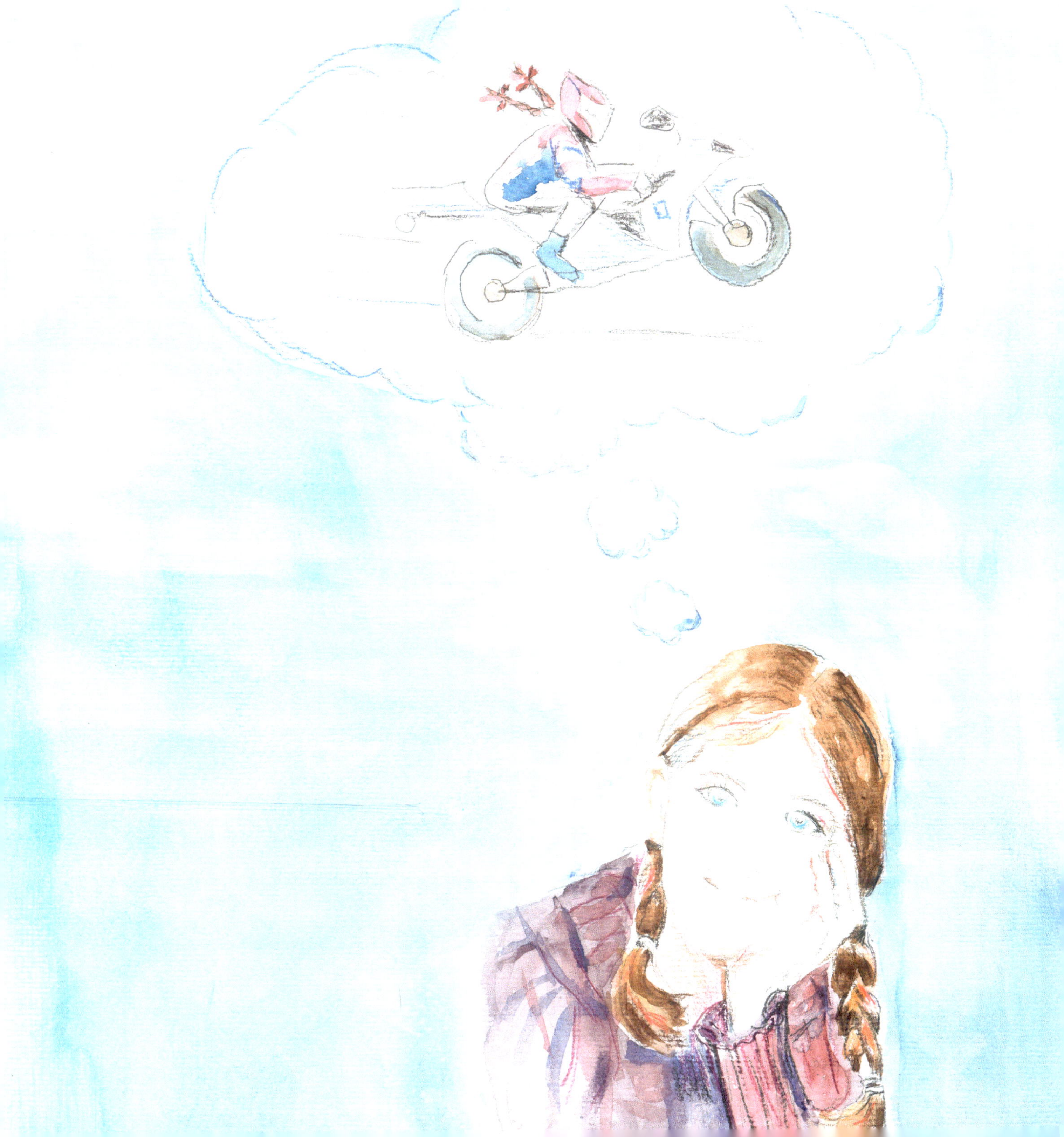

Crystal and her daddy are going to spend the summer with Granny Violet and Pappy Lee.

Granny and Pappy live in the town of
Sturgis, South Dakota.

Crystal gets ready for bed. Chaps look great
with pajamas.

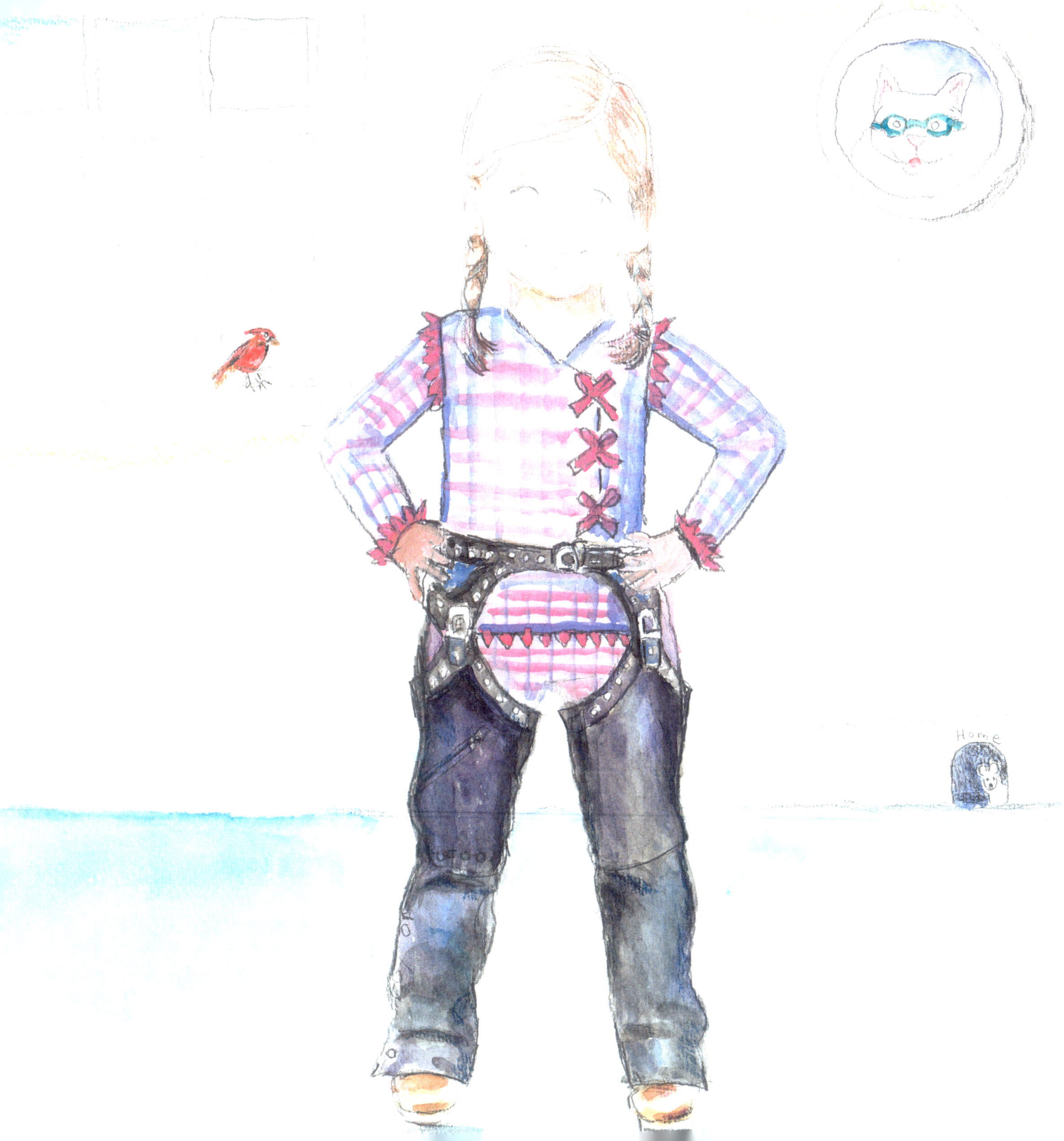
Home

The next morning
Crystal puts on
the rest of her
motorcycle outfit.
She dresses Roger the dog.
Her daddy tells her that Roger
will be going to Granny's
next week with Uncle Kevin.
She wishes Roger the dog
could go with them now.

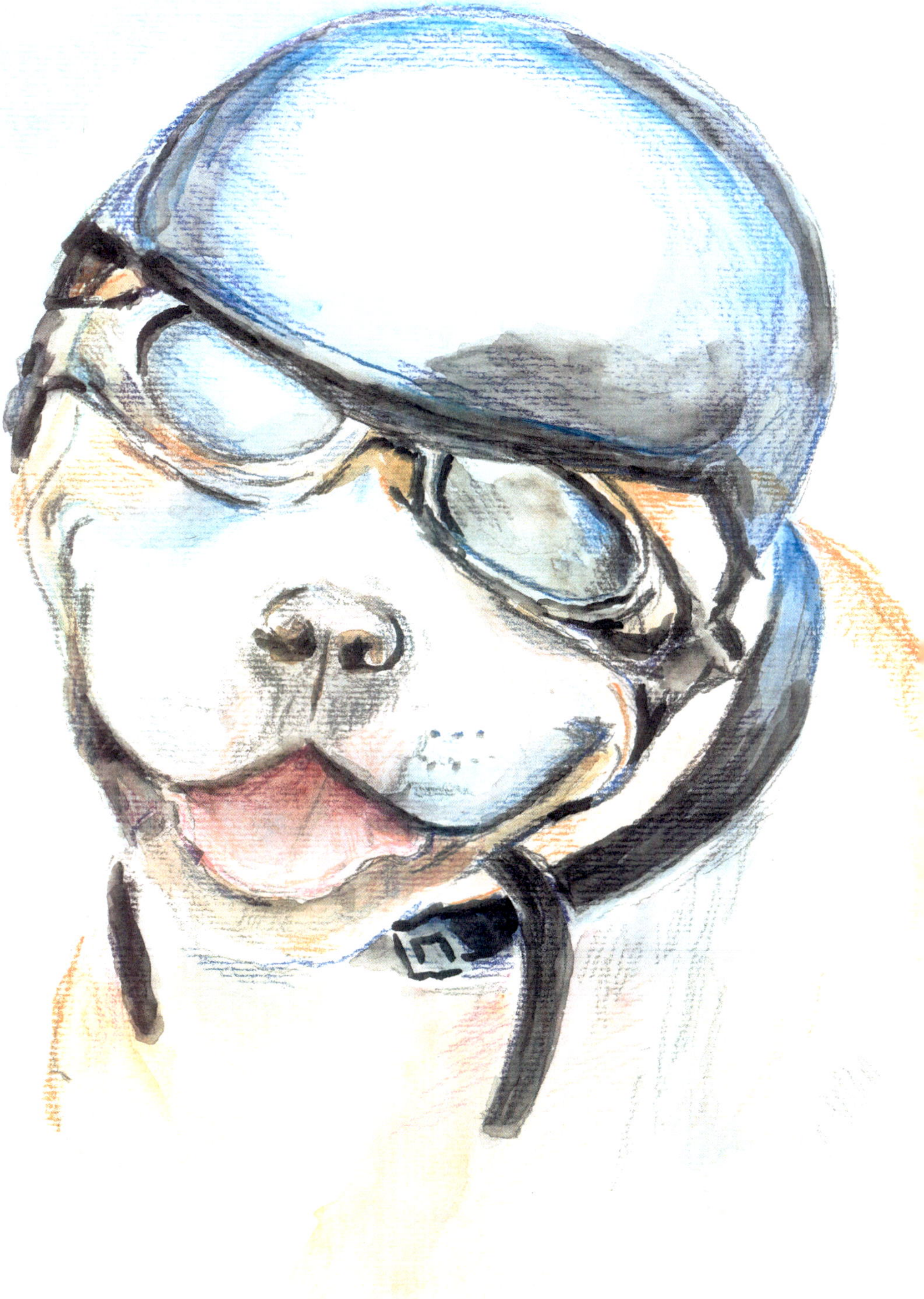

Crystal packs a lot of snacks for the trip.

Popcorn is not a good choice while riding in the sidecar.

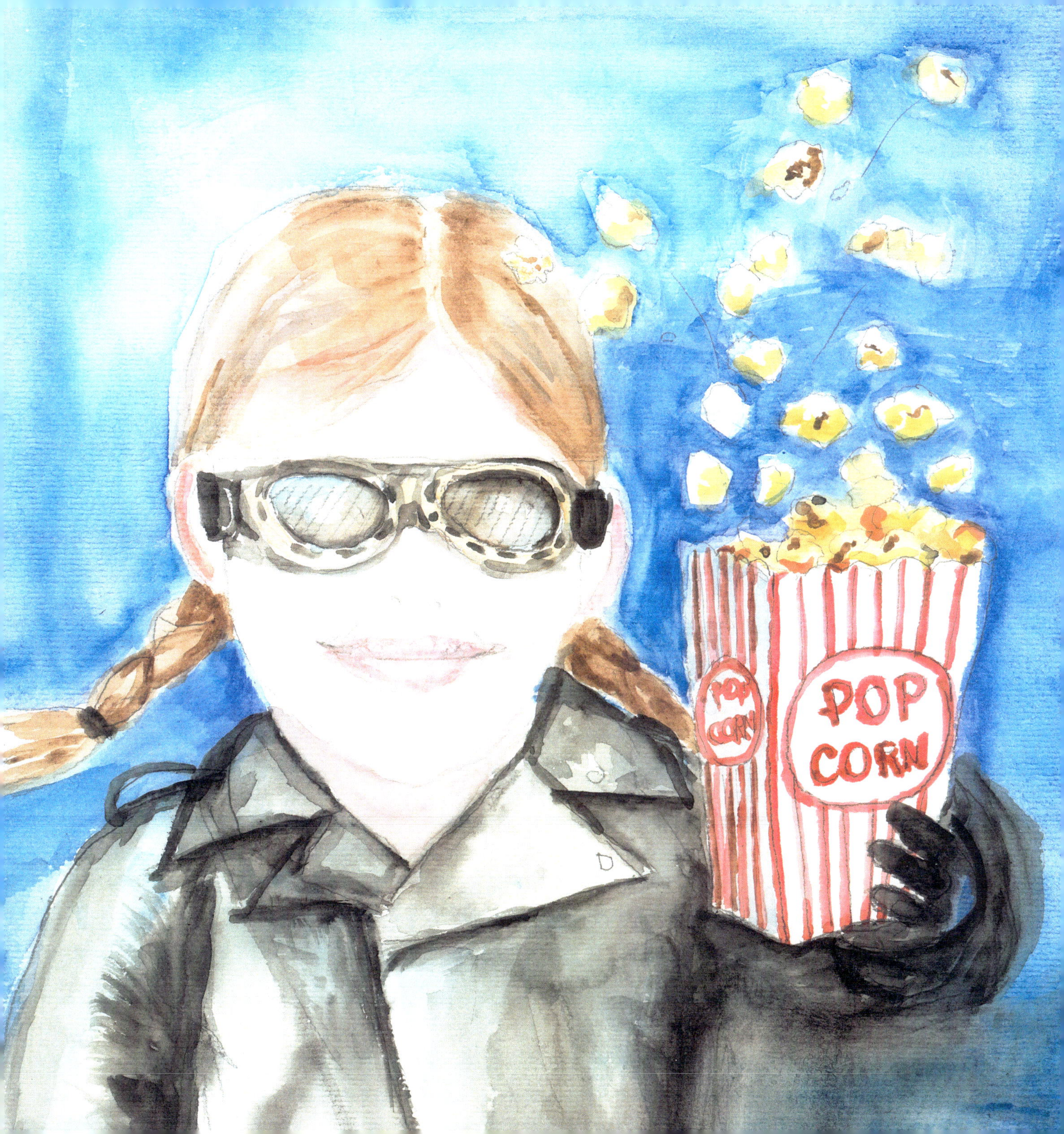
POP CORN
POP CORN

After a long day,
they stop at a campground.
Crystal hears a noise
in the middle of the night.

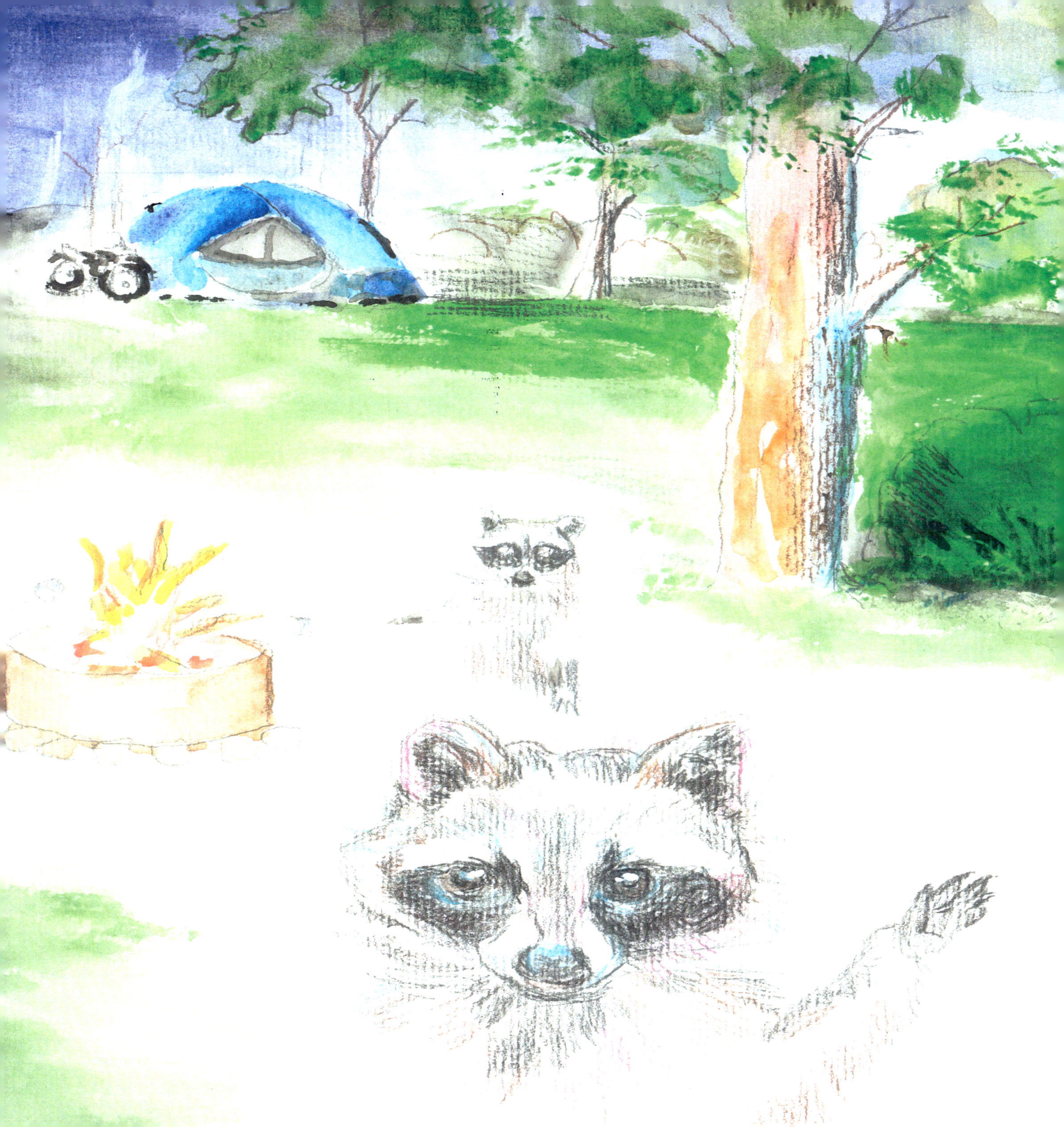

On the second day of their road trip, Crystal's daddy stops to take a picture.

There are so many wonderful things to see. Crystal likes the mountain with the heads. She is still thinking about Roger the dog.

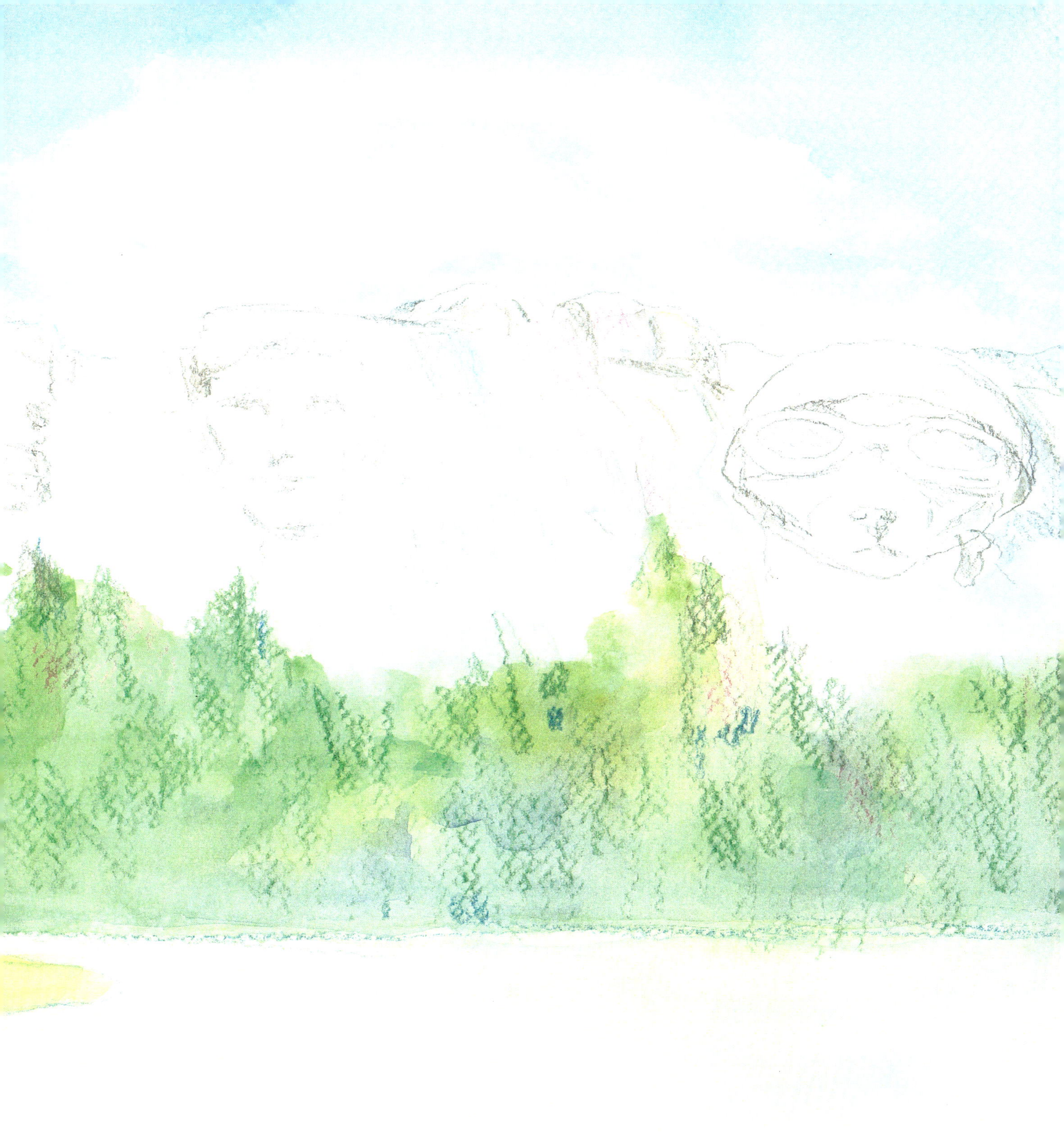

A few miles from Sturgis, they stop at a store called Millie's Trading Post. Outside the store is a large buffalo inside a fence.

Crystal stares at a picture hanging on the wall inside the store.

Daddy buys a fancy headdress for Crystal.

After a fun ride,
Crystal and her daddy
reach Sturgis.
They pull up in front of
Pappy Lee's motorcycle shop.
Crystal's daddy will spend the
summer helping pappy get
ready for the
big motorcycle rally.

Sturgis

A shiny new motorcycle pulls up beside them.

It is Pappy Lee!!

Crystal likes his helmet.

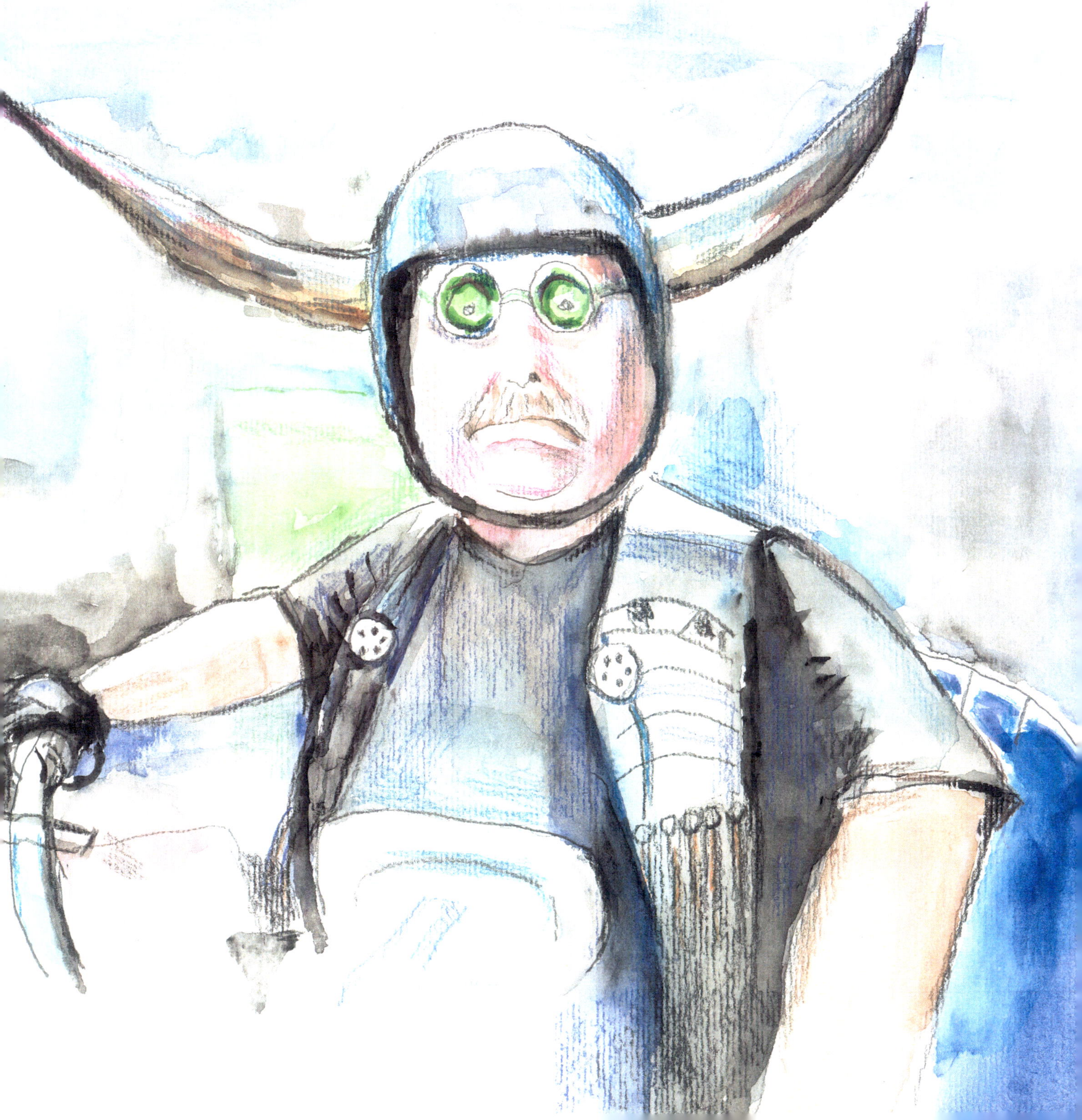

On the ride over to Granny's house, Crystal wonders what the town would look like during the rally. She thinks it would look like Paris.

STURGIS
RALLY

Granny is waiting
on the porch.
She says that Crystal
looks so grown-up
in her riding gear.

Crystal is very tired after the long ride.
Granny Violet kisses her goodnight
and turns out the light.

As Crystal falls asleep,
she hopes that
Roger the dog will arrive soon.
She knows that he will have
a fun ride
with Uncle Kevin.

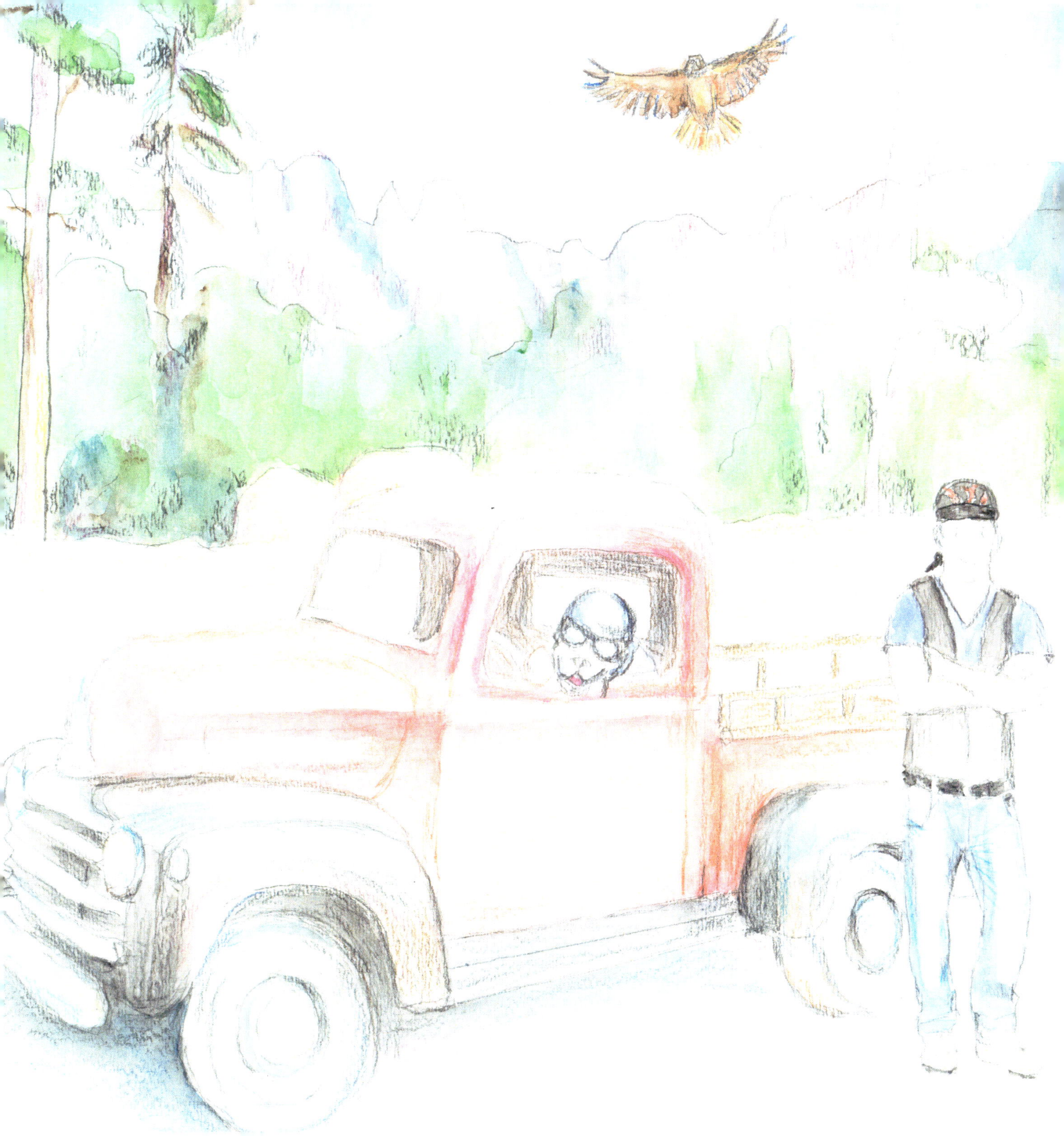

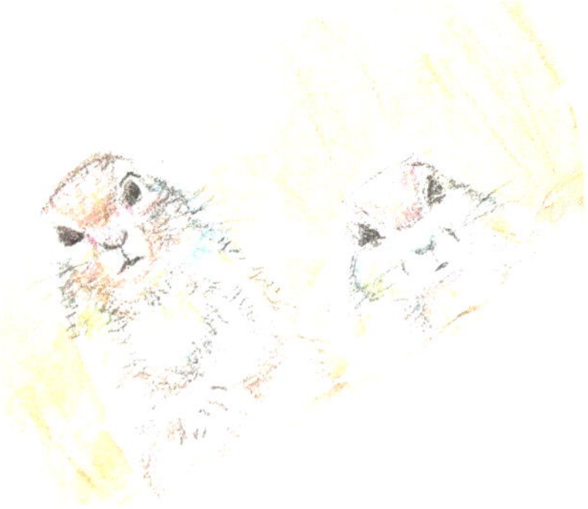

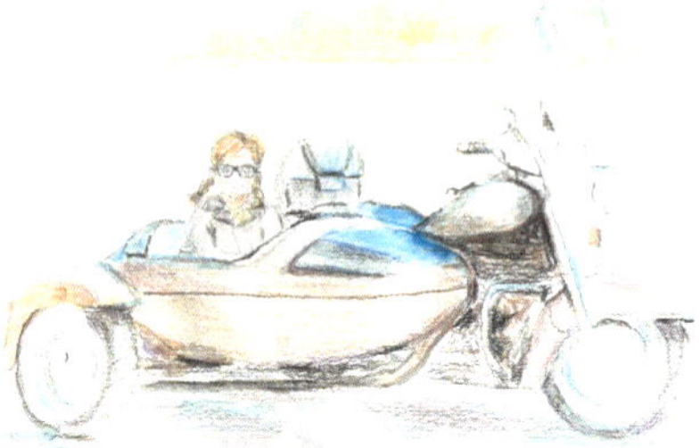

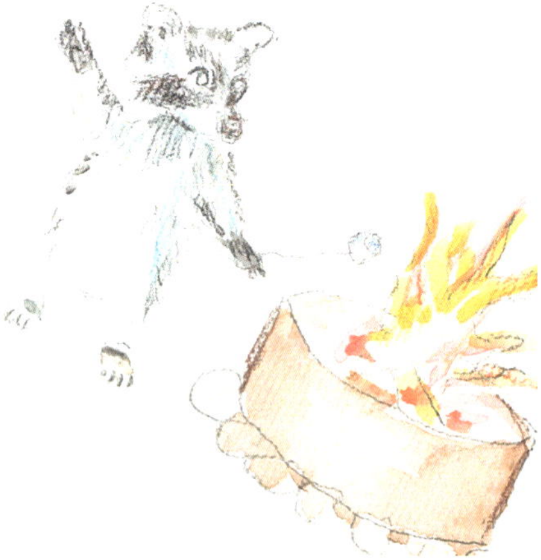

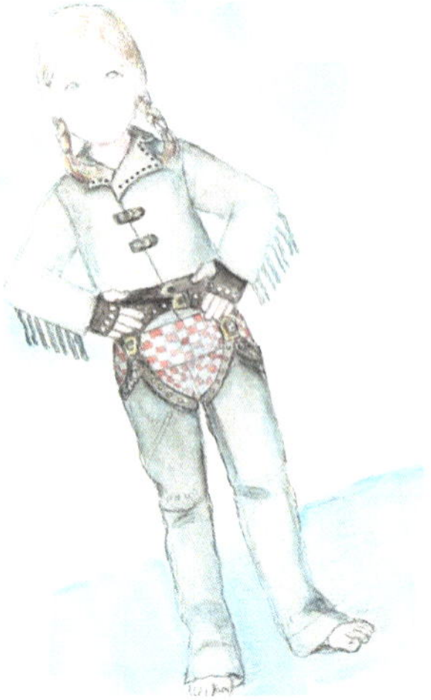

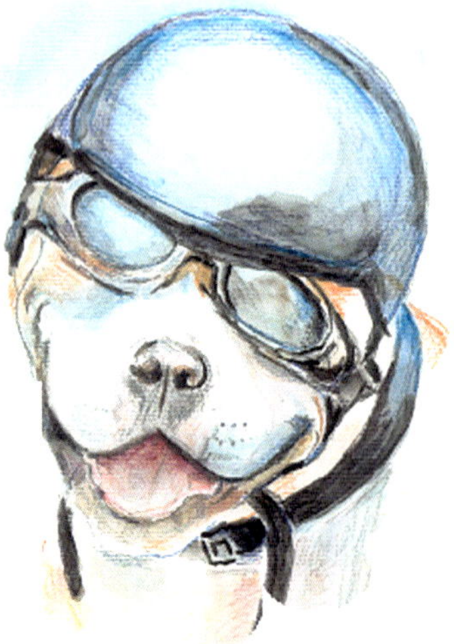

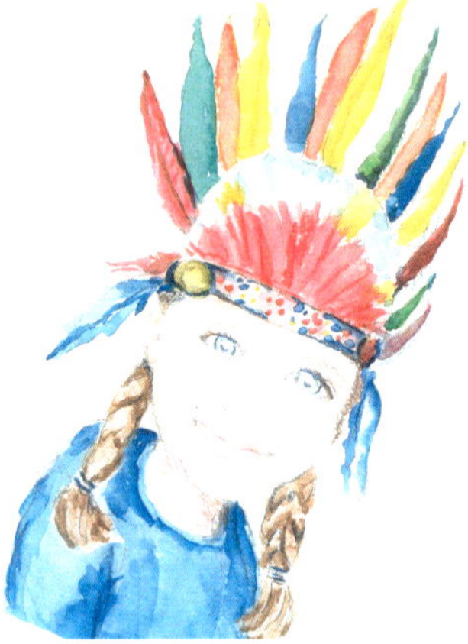

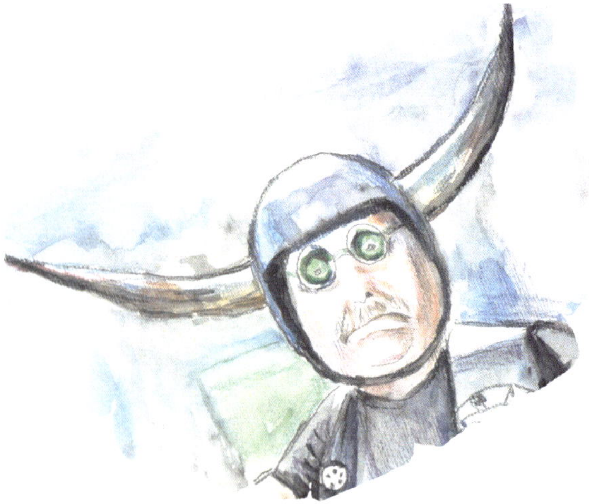

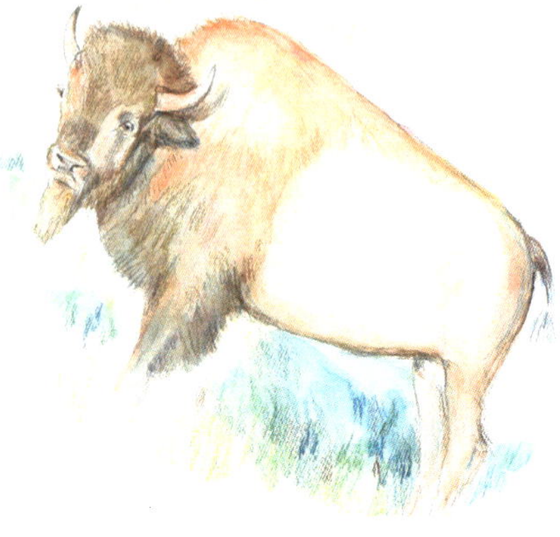